How Great Soul Winners Were Filled with the HOLY SPIRIT

GLORIOUS EXPERIENCES, TESTIMONIES AND FACTS ABOUT

D. L. Moody

R. A. Torrey

J. Wilbur Chapman

Charles H. Spurgeon

Charles G. Finney

Billy Sunday

AND MANY OTHER GREAT SOUL WINNERS, SHOWING WHAT THE FULLNESS OF THE SPIRIT MEANS AND HOW TO RECEIVE THIS POWER

by Evangelist
JOHN R. RICE, D.D., Litt.D.

Copyright 1949 by
Dr. John R. Rice
in *The Power of Pentecost*
77,000 copies printed

Price: 25¢ a copy

Life-Changing Pamphlet Library -- *John R. Rice*

Any 5 copies $1.00   25¢ PAMPHLET SERIES   Special price per hundred
(by Dr. Rice, unless otherwise indicated)

All Have Sinned
All Satan's Apples Have Worms
Attack on the Bible
Backslider, The
Balaam (Sumner)
Banquet Invitation
Bible or Evolution? (Bryan)
Blight of Booze (Sumner)
Can a Saved Person Ever Be Lost?
Christ Is Coming, Signs or No Signs
Christian and War, The (Moyer)
Christmas Pageant
Christ's Literal Reign
Church Members Who Make God Sick
Churches and the Church
Come Back to Bethel
Correction and Discipline of Children
Count Your Blessings
Courtship and Dangers of Petting
Crossing the Deadline
Dangerous Triplets
David and Bath-sheba
Dear Catholic Friend
Divorce, the Wreck of Marriage
Double Curse of Booze, The
Ecumenical Folly (Weniger)
Eight Gospel Absurdities
Evolution or the Bible — Which?
Fall of a Preacher
Father, Mother, Home and Heaven
Finnish Gold Story, The (Gordon)
Four Biggest Fools in Town
Fullness of the Spirit
Giving Your Way to Prosperity
God's Authority
Good Man Lost — Bad Man Saved
Healing in Answer to Prayer
Hell! What the Bible Says About It
Hey! Young People! (Meloon)
High Cost of Revival, The
Hindrances to Prayer

House-to-House Soul Winning (Malone)
How God Blessed a Young Evangelist (Sumner)
How Great Soul Winners Were Filled
How Jesus, Our Pattern
Jehoshaphat's Sin
Jesus May Come Today!
Last Judgment of the Unsaved Dead
Let's Baptize More Converts (Hyles)
Lot
Missing God's Last Train
Neglect, Shortest Way to Hell
Negro and White
Never Alone, Never Forsaken
Our God-Breathed Book, the Bible
Personal Soul Winning
Rebellious Wives and Slacker Husbands
Religious But Lost
Saved For Certain
Seeing Him Who Is Invisible (Hyles)
Separation (Sumner)
Sermon From a Catholic Bible
Sex Education (Hyles)
Soul Winning
Spectators at the Cross
Storehouse Tithing
Sunday or Sabbath
Sword Special Songs
Tears in Heaven
Tobacco: Is Its Use a Sin?
Trailed by a Wild Beast
Unequal Yoke, The
Verbal Inspiration
War in Vietnam
What Is a Jehovah's Witness? (Wimbish)
What Was Back of Kennedy's Murder?
What Will Happen When Jesus Comes?
Why Preach Against Sin?
"Woman Thou Gavest Me, The"
Wonderful Jesus
Worst Thing That Can Happen (Sumner)

Order from your bookseller or from

Sword of the Lord   Box 1099, Murfreesboro, Tenn. 37130

Printed in U. S. A.

How Great Soul Winners Were Filled With the Holy Spirit

"But ye shall receive power, after that the Holy Ghost is come upon you: and ye shall be witnesses unto me both in Jerusalem, and in all Judaea, and in Samaria, and unto the uttermost part of the earth." —Acts 1:8

". . In the mouth of two or three witnesses shall every word be established." —II Cor. 13:1

SOMEONE HAS SAID that one example is worth a thousand arguments. We do not believe that one human illustration is worth more than any statement of Scripture, and yet illustrations help us to understand the statements of Scripture; and often one illustration does more to show what the Bible really means by what it says than much human logical explanation.

It is not wise to base a doctrine upon human experiences. For example, thousands of people have been converted to God, really saved, at mourners' benches. But that is not any reason for anybody to say that a mourners' bench is essential to salvation. Some people delight in their "experience," remembering that they felt a great ecstasy and shouted the praises of God when they were born again. But it would be foolish for us to thereby conclude that one cannot be saved without shouting the praises of God. It is never wise to make a doctrine out of our human experiences. Nevertheless, when the Bible clearly teaches a truth, it is refreshing and helpful to have human experiences testify to the truth of the Bible doctrine. So in this chapter I want to tell the story of how great soul winners were filled with the Holy Spirit. And we will find that the experiences of the greatest soul winners verify the clear statements of Jesus Christ in Acts 1:8, given above. When great men of God were filled with the Holy Spirit they received power for soul-winning witness and testimony. The best soul winners did not talk in tongues, they did not claim to have the carnal nature eradicated, but they did receive power from God for soul-winning work.

In that great book, *The Holy Spirit: Who He Is, and What He Does*, Dr. R. A. Torrey in chapter five gives three defining statements as to what the baptism of the Holy Spirit is. So, before we consider the experiences of great soul winners and how they were filled with the Spirit, let us consider Dr. Torrey's definition. Dr. Torrey says the following:

1. In the first place, the Baptism of the Holy Spirit is a definite experience of which one may know whether he has received it or not....

2. In the second place, the Baptism with the Holy Spirit is a work of the Holy Spirit distinct from and additional to His regenerating work....

3. In the third place, the Baptism with the Holy Spirit is a work of the Holy Spirit always connected with and primarily for the purpose of testimony and service.

While we do not insist on the term, "the Baptism with the Holy Spirit," we believe Dr. Torrey has given a good definition of this special enduement of power from on high. With this in mind, we will do well to consider the testimonies of great men who were filled with the Holy Spirit and see that the fullness of the Holy Spirit is indeed a special enduement of power fitting Christians to win souls, and we will see how other Christians received this enduement of power.

D. L. Moody's Enduement

In *The Life of D. L. Moody,* written by his son, is a very simple but striking account of the secret of D. L. Moody's power. Here is the story of Mr. Moody's enduement of power, as given on pages 146, 147, and 149.

The year 1871 was a critical one in Mr. Moody's career. He realized more and more how little he was fitted by personal acquirements for his work. An intense hunger and thirst for spiritual power were aroused in him by two women who used to attend the meetings and sit on the front seat. He could see by the expression on their faces that they were praying. At the close of services they would say to him:

"We have been praying for you."

"Why don't you pray for the people?" Mr. Moody would ask.

"Because you need the power of the Spirit," they would say.

"I need the power! Why," said Mr. Moody, in relating the incident years after, "I thought I had power. I had the largest congregations in Chicago, and there were many conversions. I was in a sense satisfied. But right along those two godly women kept praying for me, and their earnest talk about anointing for special service set me to thinking. I asked them to come and talk with me, and they poured out their hearts in prayer that I might receive the filling of the Holy Spirit. There came a great hunger into my soul. I did not know what it was. I began to cry out as I never did before. I really felt that I did not want to live if I could not have this power for service."

Then the book tells of the great Chicago fire, of D. L. Moody's relief work, the building of the north side tabernacle, and of his visiting in the East to secure funds for his work. Then the narrative continues:

During this Eastern visit the hunger for more spiritual power was still upon Mr. Moody.

"My heart was not in the work of begging," he said. "I could not appeal. I was crying all the time that God would fill me with His Spirit. Well, one day, in the city of New York—oh, what a day!— I cannot describe it, I seldom refer to it; it is almost too sacred an experience to name. Paul had an experience of which he never spoke for fourteen years. I can only say that God revealed Himself to me, and I had such an experience of His love that I had to ask Him to stay His hand. I went to preaching again. The sermons were not different; I did not present any new truths, and yet hundreds were converted. I would not now be placed back where I was before that blessed experience if you should give me all the world—it would be as the small dust of the balance."

Notice in the above account, in the words of D. L. Moody himself, that while he had great joy in the coming of the Holy Spirit upon him in power, yet the principal result was: "The sermons were not different: I did not present any new truths, and yet hundreds were converted."

D. L. Moody himself made much of this doctrine that Christians should be filled with the Holy Spirit, or baptized with the Holy Spirit, as he himself often put it.

In the book, *Moody, His Words, Work, and Workers,* edited by Rev. W. H. Daniels, are given representative doctrinal messages by D. L. Moody. I want to quote here from one message, beginning on page 396 of that book, to show Moody's clear doctrine on this matter of an enduement of power from on high.

D. L. Moody's Article on
THE BAPTISM OF THE HOLY SPIRIT FOR SERVICE

In some sense, and to some extent, the Holy Spirit dwells with every believer; but there is another gift, which may be called the gift of the Holy Spirit for service. This gift, it strikes me, is entirely distinct and separate from conversion and assurance. God has a great many children that have no power, and the reason is, they have not the gift of the Holy Ghost for service. God doesn't seem to work with them, and I believe it is because they have not sought this gift.

In the opening of the eleventh chapter of Luke we find the disciples asking Christ to teach them how to pray. After doing so he goes on to explain it, and in the ninth, tenth, and thirteenth verses says: "And I say unto you, Ask, and it shall be given you; seek, and ye shall find; knock, and it shall be opened unto you. For every one that asketh receiveth. . . . If ye then, being evil, know how to give good gifts unto your children; how much more shall your heavenly Father give the Holy Spirit to them that ask him!"

Now the lesson to be learned from this is, that we must pray for the Holy Spirit for service; pray that we may be anointed and qualified to do the work that God has for us to do. I believe that Elisha was a child of God before Elijah met him; but he was not qualified for the work of a prophet until the spirit of Elijah came upon him. We have to ask for this blessing, to knock for it, to seek for it, and find out why it does not come. If we regard iniquity in our hearts, if we have some hidden sin, God is not going to give us the baptism of power. We are not as "an empty vessel"; we are not ready to receive the blessing, and so it doesn't come.

In the third chapter of Luke we find that Christ was baptized by the Holy Ghost before he entered upon his ministry. This should teach us to get anointed before starting out to do the Lord's work. Christ was the Son of God just as much before his baptism as afterward, but even he needed this power; and if the Son of God, who never had sinned, needed it, how much more do we need it, and how hopeless it will be if we attempt to work before we get it.

Again you will notice Mr. Moody's teaching that the coming of the Holy Spirit upon Christians, what Moody and Torrey and most other great soul winners have called "the baptism of the Holy Spirit," is simply an enduement of power for soul-winning service; that Christians should pray for this enduement of power from on high.

That Moody's work was done in the mighty power of the Holy Spirit, that he really had upon him the power of Pentecost, was obvious to all who knew him well. At Moody's funeral C. I. Scofield, then about 56 years old, spoke. And though later —when there was such a hue and cry raised by the followers of Darby against the terminology of Moody and Torrey and other great soul winners on this matter of the baptism of the Holy Spirit, or the fullness of the Spirit—Scofield avoided it, yet on this occasion he used the terminology of Moody and of Torrey and of Finney. Here are Dr. Scofield's words over the body of the great soul winner, Moody:

The secrets of Dwight L. Moody's power were: First, in a definite experience of Christ's saving grace. He had passed out of death into life, and he knew it. Secondly, he believed in the divine authority of the Scriptures. The Bible was to him the voice of God, and he made it resound as such in the consciences of men. *Thirdly, he was baptized with the Holy Spirit, and he knew it.* [Italics supplied] It was to him as definite an experience as his conversion (*The Life of D. L. Moody* by his son, page 561).

Oh, how earnest was Moody in his burden to keep the power of the Spirit of God upon him! He said once, in his sermon on "Hindered Power," in the book, *Secret Power*, "I have lived long enough to know that if I cannot have the power of the Spirit of God on me to help me to work for Him, I would rather die, than to live just for the sake of living."

In Dr. R. A. Torrey's great message on *Why God Used D. L. Moody*, he named seven qualities that made Moody the wonderfully used man that he was. And the seventh, last and most important was that Moody was "definitely endued with power from on high." Listen to what R. A. Torrey said (pages 51-55) about Mr. Moody:

The seventh thing that was the secret of why God used D. L. Moody was that, *he had a very definite enduement with power from on high*, a very clear and definite *baptism with the Holy Ghost*. Mr. Moody knew he had the "baptism with the Holy Ghost"; he had no doubt about it. In his early days he was a great hustler, he had a tremendous desire to do something, but he had no real power. He worked very largely in the energy of the flesh. But there were two humble Free Methodist women who used to come over to his meetings in the Y.M.C.A. One was "Auntie Cook" and the other Mrs. Snow. (I think her name was not Snow at that time.) These two women would come to Mr. Moody at the close of his meetings and say: "We are praying for you." Finally, Mr. Moody became somewhat nettled and said to them one night: "Why are you praying for me? Why don't you pray for the unsaved?" They replied: "We are praying that you may get the power." Mr. Moody did not know what that meant, but he got to thinking about it, and then went to these women and said: "I wish you would tell me what you mean," and they told him about the definite baptism with the Holy Ghost. Then he asked that he might pray with them and not they merely pray for him.

Auntie Cook once told me of the intense fervour with which Mr. Moody prayed on that occasion. She told me in words that I scarcely dare repeat, though I have never forgotten them. And he not only prayed with them, but he also prayed alone. Not long after, one day on his way to England, he was walking up Wall Street in New York (Mr. Moody very seldom told this and I almost hesitate to tell it) and in the midst of the bustle and hurry of that city his prayer was answered; the power of God fell upon him as he walked up the street and he had to hurry off to the house of a friend and ask that he might have a room by himself, and in that room he stayed alone for hours; and the Holy Ghost came upon him filling his soul with such joy that at last he had to ask God to withhold His hand, lest he die on the spot from very joy. He went out from that place with the power of the Holy Ghost upon him, and when he got to London (partly through the prayers of a bedridden saint in Mr. Lessey's church) the power of God wrought through him mightily in North London and hundreds were added to the churches, and that was what led to his being invited over to the wonderful campaign that followed in later years.

Time and again Mr. Moody would come to me and say: "Torrey, I want you to preach on baptism with the Holy Ghost." I do not know how many times he asked me to speak on that subject. Once, when I had been invited to preach in the Fifth Avenue Presbyterian Church, New York (invited at Mr. Moody's suggestion; had it not been for his suggestion the invitation would never have been extended to me), just before I started for New York, Mr. Moody drove up to my house and said: "Torrey, they want you to preach at the Fifth Avenue Presbyterian Church in New York. It is a great, big church, cost a million dollars to build it." Then he continued: "Torrey, I just want to ask one thing of you. I want to tell you what to preach about. You will preach that sermon of yours on 'Ten Reasons Why I Believe the Bible to Be the Word of God' and your sermon on 'The Baptism With the Holy Ghost.'" Time and again, when a call came to me to go off to some church, he would come up to me and say: "Now, Torrey, be sure and preach on the baptism with the Holy Ghost."

Oh, if we had more men filled with the Holy Spirit, endued with power from on high as Moody was, we would have more men showing Moody's results!

R. A. Torrey Was Definitely Filled With the Holy Ghost for Soul-Winning Power

Already you know, by what Dr. Torrey said about D. L. Moody, that he believed, as Moody did, that one to win souls for Christ must have the power of God, a special enduement of power, that is, must be filled with the Spirit of God. Torrey was in some sense the successor of D. L. Moody. He was certainly Moody's most trusted helper. In one world-wide tour R. A. Torrey's campaigns resulted in a hundred thousand souls saved. So says George T. B. Davis in his book, *Twice Around the World With Alexander*. Mr. Davis says that Torrey and Alexander were the "successors of Moody and Sankey." Telling of Torrey's and Alexander's campaigns in England, Davis said, "In Birmingham during a single month's campaign 7,700 confessed

Christ; while in London, in a five months' Mission, held in Royal Albert Hall, England's finest auditorium, and in two specially erected iron buildings, about 17,000 made public profession. In all, during the three years' work in the British Isles, about 80,000 converts were recorded . . ." Thousands of others were saved in Australia; and of course many, many thousands in campaigns in America. So the scholarly Torrey walked in the steps of the uneducated Moody. Both of them alike were filled with the Holy Spirit. And let us read what Dr. Torrey says about himself.

In his book, *The Holy Spirit: Who He Is, and What He Does*, in the chapter, "The Baptism With the Holy Spirit," pages 107-108, Dr. Torrey says:

The address of this afternoon, and the addresses of the days immediately to follow, are the outcome of an experience, and that experience was the outcome of a study of the Word of God. After I had been a Christian for some years, and after I had been in the ministry for some years, my attention was strongly attracted to certain phrases found in the Gospels and in the Acts of the Apostles, and in the Epistles, such as "baptized with the Holy Spirit," "filled with the Spirit," "the Holy Spirit fell upon them," "the gift of the Holy Spirit," "endued with power from on high," and other closely allied phrases. As I studied these various phrases in their context, it became clear to me that they all stood for essentially the same experience; and it also became clear to me that God has provided for each child of His in this present dispensation that they should be thus "baptized with the Spirit," or, "filled with the Spirit."

As I studied the subject still further, I became convinced that they described an experience which I did not myself possess, and I went to work to secure for myself the experience thus described. I sought earnestly that I might "be baptized with the Holy Spirit." I went at it very ignorantly. I have often wondered if anyone ever went at it any more ignorantly than I did. But while I was ignorant, I was thoroughly sincere and in earnest, and God met me, as He always meets the sincere and earnest soul, no matter how ignorant he may be; and God gave me what I sought, I was "baptized with the Holy Spirit." And the result was a transformed Christian life and a transformed ministry.

Torrey, too, was filled with the Holy Spirit. He did not talk in tongues, he never claimed to have the carnal nature eradicated, but he did receive a mighty enduement of power from on high. It came after he was saved and made him a mighty soul winner.

In the book, *Holiness and Power*, pages 337-338, Rev. A. M.

Hills tells of a letter from Dr. Torrey in the following words:

I wrote a letter to Brother Torrey of Chicago, a month ago, asking him to tell me how he came to seek the baptism of the Holy Spirit, and what the blessing had done for him. He replied as follows: "I was led to seek the baptism with the Holy Spirit because I became convinced from the study of the Acts of the Apostles that no one had a right to preach the gospel until he had been baptized with the Holy Spirit. At last I was led to the place where I said that I would never enter the pulpit again until I had been baptized with the Holy Ghost and knew it, or until God in some way told me to go. I obtained the blessing in less than a week. If I had understood the Bible as I do now there need not have passed any days.

"As to what the blessing has done for me, I could not begin to tell. It has brought a joy into my soul that I never dreamed of before; a liberty in preaching that makes preaching an unspeakable delight where before it was a matter of dread; it has opened to me a door of usefulness, so that now, instead of preaching to a very little church, I have calls every year to proclaim the truth to very many thousands, being invited to conventions in every part of the land to address vast audiences; and I have a church today, in addition to my work in the Institute, that has a membership of upwards of thirteen hundred, with an evening audience that sometimes overflows the auditorium of the church, into which we can pack twenty-five hundred people, into the lecture-room below."

This letter by Dr. Torrey was written before he made his world-wide tour and before he was in a life of evangelistic campaigns. Yet he knew that he had been definitely endued with power from on high. He had had a definite time of seeking the power of God and knew that he had found that which he sought. God gave him power in preaching the Word and teaching and it resulted in multitudes saved.

Dr. J. Wilbur Chapman Filled With the Holy Spirit

Rev. A. M. Hills was state evangelist in Michigan for the Congregational church. His book, *Holiness and Power*, is a good book, though we do not vouch for Brother Hills' position on holiness. But Hills tells in the following words, page 336, of a time when Dr. J. Wilbur Chapman went before God and sought His power and found it:

Dr. Wilbur Chapman tells us how he went before God and consecrated himself and then said in faith, "My Father, I now claim from Thee the infilling of the Holy Ghost," and he says: "From that moment to this He has been a living reality. I never knew what it was to love my family before. I never knew what it was to study the Bible before. And why should I, for had I not just then found the key? I never knew what it was to preach before. 'Old things have passed away' in my experience. 'Behold all things have become new.'"

Even more revealing of Dr. Chapman's teaching and practice and experience in the power of the Holy Spirit is the following passage by Dr. Chapman:

"I had," said Dr. Chapman, "an ignorant man in my church, in Philadelphia, by the name of S., who utterly murdered the king's English. When he first stood up to talk, and you heard him for the first time, you would be amazed, and would hope that he would not speak long. But soon you would begin to wonder at the marvelous power of his words. I will tell you the secret of it. I once called thirty of the workers of my church together to pray for the baptism of power for a special work. He rose and left the room. I afterward found him alone in a little room of the church pleading in prayer: 'O Lord, take all sin from me. Teach me what it is that hinders Thy coming. I will give up everything. Come, O Holy Spirit, come and take possession of me, and help me to win men.' He arose from his knees and met me face to face, and said: 'Pastor, I have received the Holy Ghost.' To my certain knowledge, since that time (about three years) that ignorant man has led more than a hundred men to Jesus." (*Holiness and Power*, pages 329-30).

The marvelous ministry of J. Wilbur Chapman can be explained only by the fact that he, like Moody and Torrey, was filled with the Holy Spirit, definitely endued with the Holy Spirit, or filled with the Holy Spirit, or baptized with the Holy Spirit, whichever term you care to use. Chapman was associated with Moody, was selected by Moody to be vice-president of Moody Bible Institute and was the author of the book, *The Life and Work of D. L. Moody*. In fact, Dr. Chapman tells us that it was Moody himself who led Chapman to the first full assurance of salvation.

In the biography of J. Wilbur Chapman by Ottman, is this striking statement: "He had witnessed such marvelous manifestations of the Spirit of God in so many of his meetings that he felt a keen disappointment when the tide failed to reach the full flood." He was a mighty, heart-moving preacher, filled with the Holy Ghost. Chapman himself had prayed for the fullness of the Spirit. He taught others to pray for "the baptism of power for a special work."

Billy Sunday, Who Won Over a Million Souls to Christ, Was Definitely Filled With the Holy Spirit

Mr. Homer Rodeheaver, Billy Sunday's song leader for the

most powerful years of his ministry, has the following to say about Mr. Sunday:

Mr. Sunday was criticized as few men. He could stand criticism. Put the spotlight on Mr. Sunday from any point of view. The result is to expose the pitiable smallness of his critics. He did things that were epic. Under his ministry more lives were changed than by any man who has preached the gospel. More than a million men and women "hit the sawdust trail." He was responsible for multitudes of ministers, missionaries, revived churches, Bible schools, and Christian activities that reach to the four corners of the earth (*Twenty Years With Billy Sunday*, p. 24).

It seems probable that in a harder day and with greater competition, Billy Sunday won more souls than did D. L. Moody, or any other single man who ever lived, as Mr. Rodeheaver says. Again Mr. Rodeheaver says, "No doubt he spoke directly to more people in the course of his career than any other man in the world. He did this without amplifiers or mechanical devices to carry his voice" (*Twenty Years With Billy Sunday*, p. 18).

Now was Billy Sunday himself filled with the Holy Spirit? Did he have a special anointing of God, an enduement of power from on high such as made possible the ministry of Moody and of Torrey and of Chapman and of other great soul winners? Beyond any shadow of doubt, Billy Sunday did have such an enduement of power, such a definite filling of the Spirit!

When I first considered this matter I was disappointed that we did not have from Billy Sunday's lips the naming of a certain date and the description of a certain experience, when the Spirit of the Lord came upon him in a special enduement of soul-winning power. I rather wanted it down in black and white in Billy Sunday's own words, some account of a wonderful period of emotion and crisis and glory to which we could point. I do not know of any such statement by Billy Sunday or of any published record of a time when Billy Sunday was definitely endued with power. And the more I think about it and pray about it the more clearly God has seemed to speak to my heart in this matter, and to show me His infinite wisdom in not allowing us to have a definite description of the time when Sunday was first filled with the Holy Spirit. I cannot describe the first time I myself was filled with the Holy Spirit. For one thing, I began soul winning when I was fifteen years old. For another thing, I had the mighty power of God upon me in soul winning before I understood the doctrine of the Holy Spirit. I prayed for power before

I knew the Bible terminology for the power I needed and wanted. I made the surrender to the will of God and gave myself wholly to soul-winning work before I knew that these were the requirements which God made for the fullness of the Holy Spirit. So I cannot describe a certain climax and crisis of emotion and glorious assurance to mark the first time I was filled with the Holy Spirit. And the same thing seems to have been true about Billy Sunday and of thousands of other remarkable soul winners. No doubt God in His mercy wanted us to see that the evidence that He himself describes in Acts 1:8: "Ye shall receive power, after that the Holy Ghost is come upon you. . ." is enough. Soul-winning power *is* enough.

But was Billy Sunday conscious of being filled with the Holy Spirit? Did he meet the requirements for a special enduement of power as other soul winners have, the same conditions? Was he conscious of a supernatural enabling that turned the hearts of sinners to Christ when he preached? Assuredly, beyond any shadow of doubt, he not only had met God's requirements, the same requirements that other men met, and had the same supernatural enabling, the same enduement of power; but he was definitely conscious of that fullness of the Spirit and relied upon the Holy Spirit to do His wondrous pentecostal work through him, Mr. Sunday, in saving souls.

We would not need further evidence on this matter than the million souls, and more, who turned to God under Mr. Sunday's preaching. Souls are saved by the power of the Holy Spirit. No one ever wins souls through any other power. Not human zeal, not human personality, not scholarship nor even the preaching of the Word of God in human wisdom can save souls. Even of the Word of God itself we are told, "the letter killeth. . ." (II Cor. 3:6). So if I never had a word from Billy Sunday, never had any indication of his doctrinal position on this matter, I would know that Mr. Sunday was mightily filled with the Spirit of God for winning souls.

But the evidence is overwhelming that Billy Sunday knew what God's conditions were, that he consciously met those conditions, and that he knew he was supremely filled with the Spirit of God.

Remember, first, that Billy Sunday was a disciple of J. Wilbur Chapman. He worked with the famous evangelist three years when Mr. Chapman was having great union revival campaigns. Then when Billy Sunday started his own work as an evangelist, it was sermons by Dr. Chapman which he preached. "Seven sermons given him by Dr. Chapman, plus his own testimony, made the eight with which he started his evangelistic career" *(Twenty Years With Billy Sunday,* p. 21). His three years under J. Wilbur Chapman molded his doctrine on the power of the Holy Spirit just as Moody's influence molded Dr. Chapman's. Billy Sunday always gave more credit to Dr. J. Wilbur Chapman for his preaching than to anybody else. Hence, Billy Sunday believed in and preached a definite fullness of the Holy Spirit as Dr. Chapman believed and preached it.

Billy Sunday's position on this matter is made clear all the more by his own preaching. I have, for example, his printed sermons preached in the Omaha, Nebraska, campaign in 1915. He preached one time on "Have ye received the Holy Ghost since ye believed?" (Acts 19:2); once on "But tarry ye in the city of Jerusalem, until ye be endued with power from on high" (Luke 24:49); once on "But ye shall receive power, after that the Holy Ghost is come upon you: and ye shall be witnesses unto me both in Jerusalem, and in all Judaea, and in Samaria, and unto the uttermost part of the earth" (Acts 1:8); and once on "The Revival at Pentecost." Those sermons upon those texts and subjects indicate the importance Billy Sunday himself placed upon a definite enduement of power from on high for soul winning.

But there is an even more remarkable evidence that Billy Sunday felt he was endued with power from on high and that he preached in a wonderful anointing from Heaven. Every time Billy Sunday preached he opened his Bible to one text of Scripture that declares, "The Spirit of the Lord God is upon me, because the Lord hath anointed me to preach . . .", laid his sermon notes upon that Scripture and preached with the fire and power of God! On this matter Mr. Rodeheaver, his assistant for twenty years, says:

"Invariably he opened the Bible and placed his sermon notes upon the passage in Isaiah, first verse of the sixty-first chapter, which reads: 'The Spirit of the Lord is upon me; because the Lord hath anointed me to preach good tidings unto the meek; He hath sent me to bind up the broken-hearted, to proclaim liberty to the captives, and the opening of the prisons to them that are bound.'

"Many people wanted to possess the Bible Mr. Sunday had used during a campaign. When he granted the request it would be found that these pages in the book of Isaiah were almost worn out" (*Twenty Years With Billy Sunday*, by Homer Rodeheaver, p. 10).

What experience with God did Billy Sunday have that made him always open the Bible to that one verse of Scripture? What holy vow, what compact with God moved this mighty soul winner that *always* when he preached the Gospel his Bible lay open on the pulpit with these words, "The Spirit of the Lord God is upon me; because the Lord hath anointed me to preach..."? Surely Mr. Sunday *knew* beyond a shadow of doubt that the Spirit of the Lord was upon him. And he surely knew that he was anointed to preach. I have no doubt he treasured, beyond any other knowledge, the knowledge that his power was the power of God and that he dare not trifle with it. Knowing that he had a holy anointing, he pleased God instead of men, he preached without any compromise, preached in a way that offended, that cut, that burned and that assaulted and captured the castles of men's hearts for Christ. If Billy Sunday had told me with his own voice, looking me in the face, that he knew he had a definite enduement of power from God for soul winning and that it was a holy trust with which he dared not trifle but must keep its conditions always in mind, it would not be more certain in my mind than it is. When Mr. Sunday and I were on a radio program together, sat on the same platform, and were once guests at the same table he did not tell me of such a definite secret experience. But he was filled with the Holy Ghost and knew it, and claimed this as his treasure above all treasure, his one indispensable equipment for soul winning. That we certainly know by his own emphasis on the power of the Holy Spirit in his preaching and by the fact that he always opened his Bible to this one text in Isaiah 61:1 before preaching the Gospel.

Other people may not have known where Billy Sunday got his power. But he knew, he knew! And he reminded himself of the one source from which he could have blessing and power every time he ever preached! And we are justified in supposing that every time Billy Sunday opened his Bible to Isaiah 61:1 and laid it on the pulpit before him before beginning his sermon, he made a fresh covenant with God, relying upon the power of the Holy Spirit for that sermon and humbly beseeching God for His blessing. A definite enduement of power from on high is the only possible explanation of Billy Sunday's ministry.

Charles G. Finney, Mighty Soul Winner, Baptized With the Holy Ghost!

The *Autobiography of Charles G. Finney* is one of the most helpful books in print. It was one of four books that have had the greatest influence on my Christian life and ministry. The others were *George Muller of Bristol* by A. T. Pierson, *How to Pray* by R. A. Torrey and *In His Steps* or *What Would Jesus Do?* by Charles M. Sheldon. But for a pungent and powerful revelation of how God works in soul winning and revival, few if any books ever written can exceed the *Autobiography of Charles G. Finney*. Finney won multiplied thousands of souls. Although he preached in a smaller area, and though he was handicapped by some errors in theology, Finney probably had as powerful a manifestation of the power of God upon his ministry as did D. L. Moody or any other preacher since the days of Paul, and in the smaller area which he covered in his revival work a larger proportion of the population was saved than has been true, we suppose, in the ministry of any other great evangelist. How he was filled with the Holy Spirit is told on pages 19-23 of the autobiography. Elsewhere Charles G. Finney writes, as quoted by Dr. Oswald J. Smith, in *The Revival We Need*:

I was powerfully converted on the morning of the 10th of October, 1821. In the evening of the same day I received overwhelming baptisms of the Holy Ghost, that went through me, as it seemed to me, body and soul. I immediately found myself endued with such power from on high that a few words dropped here and there to individuals were the means of their immediate conversion. My words seemed to fasten like barbed arrows in the souls of men. They cut like a sword. They broke the heart like a hammer. Multitudes can attest to this. Oftentimes a word dropped without my remembering it would fasten conviction, and often result in almost immediate conversion. Sometimes I would find myself, in a great measure, empty of this power. I would go and visit, and find that I made no saving impression. I would exhort and pray, with the same result. I would then set apart a day for private fasting and prayer, fearing that this power had departed from me, and would inquire anxiously after the reason of this apparent emptiness. After humbling myself, and crying out for help, the power would return upon me with all its freshness. This has been the experience of my life.

This power is a great marvel. I have many times seen people unable to endure the Word. The most simple and ordinary statements would cut men off their seats like a sword, would take away their strength, and render them almost helpless as dead men. Several times it has been true in my experience that I could not raise my voice, or say anything in prayer or exhortation, except in the mildest manner, without overcoming them. This power seems sometimes to pervade the atmosphere of the one who is highly charged with it. Many times great numbers of persons in a community will be clothed with this power when the very atmosphere of the whole place seems to be charged with the life of God. Strangers coming into it, and passing through the place will be instantly smitten with conviction of sin and in many instances converted to Christ. When Christians humble themselves and consecrate their all afresh to Christ, and ask for this power, they will often receive such a baptism that they will be instrumental in converting more souls in one day than in all their lifetime before. While Christians remain humble enough to retain this power, the work of conversion will go on, till whole communities and regions of country are converted to Christ. The same is true of the ministry.

It is important to notice that Charles G. Finney uses the term, "baptisms of the Holy Ghost." We do not insist upon the term, but sensible people ought not to scoff at the term, a scriptural term, as understood and used by Finney, Moody, Torrey and Chapman. Note also that this fullness of the Spirit comes, says Finney, in answer to prayer. He says that when he found himself losing power, "I would then set apart a day for private fasting and prayer. . . ." Then he says, "After humbling myself, and crying out for help, the power would return upon me with all its freshness. This has been the experience of my life."

Note again that Charles G. Finney is not talking about the eradication of the carnal nature. He did not talk in tongues. He was not seeking some special feeling, though he did have a wonderful sense of God's presence upon him. He sought and found an enduement of power from on high that made him a mighty soul winner!

Charles H. Spurgeon, Spirit-Filled Soul Winner

Charles H. Spurgeon, pastor of the Metropolitan Tabernacle in London, had as profound an effect on his age as D. L. Moody. In England he was even more eminent, we suppose, than Moody was in America. It is doubtful if any man who ever lived would be a serious competitor to Spurgeon for the title of the greatest preacher since Paul. W. Robertson Nicoll says, ". . . His was a ministry unparalleled in the whole history of the Christian church. No one but Mr. Spurgeon has steadily preached for forty years and three times a week to such audiences as he commanded.

"There were hundreds of thousands who owed him their own souls."

I do not find from Mr. Spurgeon's pen a description of a certain time and crisis when he was obviously and consciously filled for the first time with the Holy Spirit. But perhaps that is well. We should do wrong to expect every man to have the same kind of experience as far as outward manifestation and feeling are concerned. More than that, we should do wrong to believe that any such conscious period of joy or perfect understanding of the fullness of God should necessarily come at once like a glory light shining from Heaven. I am as certain as I can be that the breath of God, the power of the Holy Spirit, has, in God's great mercy, been breathed upon me. Yet I cannot name the day nor describe the experience. So Spurgeon, like Billy Sunday, has left no record of the particular time when he was first mightily filled with the power of God for soul winning. Yet the mighty anointing of the Spirit was on Spurgeon. That, we know, is the only explanation for the hundreds of thousands saved under his ministry. He himself knew that, too; and many quotations from his sermons give witness to his consciousness of the Spirit's mighty power.

In the book, *Twelve Sermons on the Holy Spirit*, and in the sermon, "The Outpouring of the Holy Spirit" (p. 50), Spurgeon says:

Jesus Christ said, "Greater works than these shall ye do because I go to my Father, in order to send the Holy Spirit"; and recollect that those few who were converted under Christ's ministry, were not converted by Him, but by the Holy Spirit that rested upon Him at that time. Jesus of Nazareth was anointed of the Holy Spirit. Now then, if Jesus Christ, the great founder of our religion, needed to be anointed of the Holy Spirit, how much more our ministers?

Again in the same sermon, on page 51, Spurgeon says:

Let the preacher always confess before he preaches that he relies upon the Holy Spirit. Let him burn his manuscript and depend upon the Holy Spirit. If the Spirit does not come to help him, let him be still and let the people go home and pray that the Spirit will help him next Sunday.

And best of all, if you would have the Holy Spirit, let us meet together earnestly to pray for Him. Remember, the Holy Spirit will not come to us as a church, unless we seek Him. "For this thing will I be enquired of by the house of Israel to do it for them." "Prove me now here, saith the Lord of hosts, and see if I do not pour you out a blessing so that there shall not be room enough to receive it."

Let us meet and pray, and if God doth not hear us, it will be the first time He has broken His promise.

In the same book, in the sermon on "The Indwelling and Outflowing of the Holy Spirit" (pp. 113, 114), Spurgeon says:

But there is another thing to be done as well, and that is *to pray;* and here I want to remind you of those blessed words of the Master, "Every one that asketh receiveth; and he that seeketh findeth; and to him that knocketh it shall be opened. If a son shall ask bread of any of you that is a father, will he give him a stone? Or if he ask a fish, will he for a fish give him a serpent? Or if he shall ask an egg, will he offer him a scorpion? If ye then, being evil, know how to give good gifts unto your children: how much more shall your heavenly Father give the Holy Spirit to them that ask him?" You see, there is a distinct promise to the children of God, that their heavenly Father will give them the Holy Spirit if they ask for His power; and that promise is made to be exceedingly strong by the instances joined to it. But he says, "*How much more* shall your heavenly Father give the Holy Spirit to them that ask him?" He makes it a stronger case than that of an ordinary parent. The Lord must give us the Spirit when we ask Him, for He has herein bound Himself by no ordinary pledge. He has used a simile which would bring dishonour on His own name, and that of the very grossest kind, if He did not give the Holy Spirit to them that ask Him.

Oh, then, let us ask Him at once, with all of our hearts. Am I not so happy as to have in this audience some who will immediately ask? I pray that some who have never received the Holy Spirit at all may now be led, while I am speaking, to pray, "Blessed Spirit, visit me; lead me to Jesus." But especially those of you that are the children of God,—to you is this promise especially made. Ask God to make you all that the Spirit of God can make you, not only a satisfied believer who has drunk for himself, but a useful believer, who overflows the neighborhood with blessing. I see here a number of friends from the country who have come to spend their holiday in London. What a blessing it would be if they went back to their respective churches overflowing; for there are numbers of churches that need flooding; they are dry as a barn-floor, and little dew ever falls on them. Oh that they might be flooded!

I was delighted to find what I did not know before, that Spurgeon understood how Jesus our Saviour was filled with the Holy Spirit as our example, and how all Christ's marvelous ministry on earth was done in the power of the Holy Spirit, not in His own power. And Spurgeon, I find, understood what I had found from the Scriptures, that the parable of the importunate friend in Luke, chapter 11, begging for bread for a friend who had journeyed to the pleader's house, pictured a Christian waiting on God for the power of the Holy Spirit to carry bread for sinners!

Let us say, then, that Spurgeon was conscious of the fullness of the Holy Spirit upon himself and that he knew whence his power came. We see also that this mighty power of God came on Spurgeon in answer to pleading prayer, yea, in answer to prayer this power came again and again upon the mighty "prince of preachers."

Evan Roberts, Welsh Evangelist, Filled With the Holy Ghost

Dr. Oswald J. Smith, in his book, *The Revival We Need*, pages 42, 43, has the following quotation from Evan Roberts, Welsh evangelist:

"For thirteen years," writes Evan Roberts, "I had prayed for the Spirit; and this is the way I was led to pray. William Davies, the deacon, said one night in the society: 'Remember to be faithful. What if the Spirit descended and you were absent? Remember Thomas! What a loss he had!'

"I said to myself: 'I will have the Spirit' and through every kind of weather and in spite of all difficulties, I went to the meetings. Many times, on seeing other boys with the boats on the tide, I was tempted to turn back and join them. But, no. I said to myself: 'Remember your resolve,' and on I went. I went faithfully to the meetings for prayer throughout the ten or eleven years I prayed for a Revival. It was the Spirit that moved me thus to think."

At a certain morning meeting which Evan Roberts attended, the evangelist in one of his petitions besought that the Lord would "bend us." The Spirit seemed to say to Roberts: "That's what you need, to be bent." And thus he describes his experience: "I felt a living force coming into my bosom. This grew and grew, and I was almost bursting. My bosom was boiling. What boiled in me was that verse: 'God commending His love.' I fell on my knees with my arms over the seat in front of me; the tears and perspiration flowed freely. I thought blood was gushing forth." Certain friends approached to wipe his face. Meanwhile he was crying out, "O Lord, bend me! Bend me!" Then suddenly the glory broke.

Mr. Roberts adds: "After I was bent, a wave of peace came over me, and the audience sang, 'I hear Thy welcome voice.' And as they sang I thought about the bending at the Judgment Day, and I was filled with compassion for those that would have to bend on that day, and I wept.

"Henceforth, the salvation of souls became the burden of my heart. From that time I was on fire with a desire to go through all Wales, and if it were possible, I was willing to pay God for the privilege of going."

Note that Evan Roberts prayed for thirteen years before the mighty revival for which he prayed came, and that the fullness of the Spirit made him the great soul winner that he became.

Many Other Mighty Soul Winners Claimed to Be Definitely Filled With the Holy Spirit

We do not have space here to give accounts of all the great men of God of whom we have a record who definitely claimed that they had a mighty enduement of power from on high, which came to them aside from their conversion to Christ. Let us mention briefly some of them.

Rev. A. B. Earle, D.D., was a Baptist evangelist who began preaching in 1830. He wrote a book, *The Rest of Faith*, telling of some of his experiences. In the introduction to one of his books, Evangelist Earle said that God had enabled him to lead 157,000 souls to Christ, and Hills in his book, *Holiness and Power*, says, "A book lies before me which says that 'he had no special power as a preacher before the Holy Ghost fell upon him.'" Dr. Earle came before D. L. Moody, but was a union evangelist wonderfully blessed of God. And he attributed his power to a definite enduement from Heaven, the fullness of the Holy Spirit for soul winning.

Mr. Hills says of A. T. Pierson, "Dr. A. T. Pierson preached eighteen years trusting to literary power and oratory and culture. He then sought and obtained 'holiness and power' by the baptism of the Holy Spirit. He afterward testified to a body of ministers: 'Brethren, I have seen more conversions and accomplished more in the eighteen months since I received that blessing than in the eighteen years previous.'" (*Holiness and Power*, page 336). And those who know the writings of Dr. Pierson will understand that he did not mean that he had had the carnal nature eradicated, nor that he had talked in tongues, but that he received power from on high for winning souls.

How many more greatly used men of God, anointed soul winners, have testified that they had a definite time, in response to earnest prayer for the power of God in soul winning, when they were filled with the Holy Spirit. There was Christmas Evans, the one-eyed Welsh evangelist wonderfully filled with the Spirit after three hours of pleading with God. There was Len G. Broughton, Southern Baptist pastor whose ministry was transformed one night as he knelt at an altar and pleaded with God for the fullness of the Spirit and claimed that power and went back to baptize three hundred converts within the year and began a marvelously increased ministry of soul winning. There was "Praying Hyde," the missionary to India. As he sailed from America a friend handed him a sealed note which he later found said, "Are you filled with the Holy Spirit?" He was first angry, then troubled, and then sought God with all of his heart until he was wonderfully filled. Great revivals with the winning of thousands of souls in India resulted. There was Dr. L. R. Scarborough, president of the Southwestern Baptist Theological Seminary, who had won twenty thousand souls for Christ and taught in our class on evangelism the need for a definite enduement of power from on high, a fullness of the Holy Spirit, which he himself had definitely received.

Mighty Lessons From the Testimony of These Spirit-Filled Giants

Every reader who is familiar with the history of great revival movements in modern times must be impressed with the fact that we have in this chapter given the position and testimony of all the mightiest soul winners—Moody, Torrey, Chapman, Sunday, Finney, Spurgeon. Who else was of their stature in revivals and soul winning? Other mighty men organized much, built great denominations, founded great schools: but the men we have named in this chapter won more souls and preached with more power than any men who have lived since the Apostle Paul, as far as we know. And it seems wonderful, to me, that these spiritual giants, manifestly filled with the power of God, were all united on the essential facts regarding the fullness of the Holy Spirit, or baptism of the Spirit, the mighty anointing of God, the power of Pentecost.

Some of the men named were better theologians than others. Some had better education than others. But all of them were mightily filled with the power of God and knew how they were filled. And all of them were agreed on the essentials of this power of Pentecost. Notice, then, some lessons from the testimony of these mighty men.

1. All of them believed that the fullness of the Holy Spirit as experienced by Christians in the book of Acts is for us today! In fact, each claimed for himself and offered for his hearers the power of the Holy Spirit.

2. All of them, without exception, believed that the fullness of the Holy Spirit was given for soul-winning power.

3. Every one of these mighty men believed that the power

of Pentecost, the fullness of the Holy Spirit, came in answer to prevailing prayer.

4. How many of these soul winners, the greatest of these twenty centuries, believed that speaking in tongues was the necessary sign of the baptism of the Holy Spirit? Not a one of them! None of them "spoke in tongues" and none of them preached that speaking in tongues was necessary or desirable as a sign of the fullness of the Holy Spirit!

5. None of the greatest soul winners of the centuries claimed the eradication of the carnal nature nor that the baptism of the Holy Spirit brought sinlessness! Charles G. Finney later taught a doctrine of sanctification but never did claim that his own mighty baptism with the Spirit (that is what he called it) made him sinless or eradicated the carnal nature at the time. (See his autobiography.) Even John Wesley, whose testimony is not given here, did not develop his idea of Christian perfection until long after he himself had his wonderful Aldersgate experience with the Holy Spirit.

I believe that the experience and the testimony of the mighty men of God whose words we have given in this chapter are overwhelming in their unity. Let no one think that the doctrine of this book is new or strange. Essentially it is the same as the teaching of Spurgeon, Moody, Torrey, Chapman, Sunday, Finney, Christmas Evans, A. T. Pierson, Len G. Broughton, "Praying Hyde," A. B. Earle, and L. R. Scarborough.

Those who have gone away from the doctrine of the fullness of the Spirit, the power of Pentecost, as a special enduement of power for soul winning possible for every Christian and to be sought with prevailing prayer, have departed from the position of the great soul winners. This falling away in doctrine came with the falling away from revival! Men do not believe in the power of Pentecost simply because they do not themselves have the power of Pentecost.

I leave this subject feeling that every reader will be held accountable to God for what he does about the overwhelming testimony of the great soul-winning giants of the centuries who say that they themselves were mightily filled with the Holy Spirit for soul winning, and in answer to prayer, and that this mighty enduement of power did not cause them to speak in tongues, did not eradicate the carnal nature. May God speak to every humble heart who reads and make him willing to receive the testimony of those upon whom God has breathed in His mighty power.

DO YOU HAVE THE POWER YOU NEED?

THE POWER OF PENTECOST
or
The Fullness of the Spirit

By JOHN R. RICE, D.D., Litt.D.

• • • The result of seventeen years of loving labor, by Dr. Rice, author of scores of helpful books and booklets. Here is the most important book on this subject to appear in 20 years.

Chapter Titles

1. The Lost Secret-Power
2. The Usual Work of the Holy Spirit
3. Jesus, Filled With the Holy Ghost
4. Misunderstood Pentecost
5. Spirit-Filled Means Empowered Witnessing
6. Bible Terminology for the Power of Pentecost
7. The Fullness of the Holy Spirit and the Ministry Gifts in Old Testament and New
8. Speaking with Tongues
9. The Power of Pentecost for Every Christian
10. How to Be Filled With the Holy Spirit
11. Prayer—A Condition of Holy Spirit Fullness
12. Why Prevailing, Persistent Praying Is Necessary for Holy Spirit Power
13. Do You Really Want to Be Spirit-Filled?
14. How Great Soul Winners Were Filled With the Holy Spirit
15. Claim Your Blessing

If you have enjoyed reading the booklet, "How Great Soul Winners Were Filled With the Holy Spirit," you will enjoy the larger book from which it is reprinted.

The largest and most exhaustive study in print on soul-winning power. Full explanation of Pentecost: I Corinthians, chapter 14. Not the new teaching of the Darbyites and ultradispensationalists, but the old-time teaching of Moody, Torrey, Spurgeon, Finney.

A book of ripest scholarship, it avoids the pitfalls of false cults and extremists. No fanaticism. Solid Bible teaching, fervent, Spirit-filled application, quotations from famous Christians. Here you may actually learn what the fullness of the Spirit means, what it will do for you, how to have it.

441 pages, detailed indexing, beautifully bound. An important book for every soul winner and Christian worker. Price . . . $4.25

Order from your bookseller or from
SWORD OF THE LORD PUBLISHERS
Box 1099, Murfreesboro, Tenn. 37130

CPSIA information can be obtained
at www.ICGtesting.com
Printed in the USA
LVHW090955080219
606884LV00003B/6/P